The National Extraordinary Professional Women

Mrs. Diane Winbush founder

Table of Contents

1. Board of Directors

2. Welcome from the Founder

3. Mission Statement

4. Services

5. Advertising Opportunities

6. Advertising Rates

7. Disclaimer

8. A Letter from the Founder

9. Notes

10. My Journal

11. Record your Networks

The National Extraordinary Professional Women

Celebrating WOMEN TRANSFORMING LIVES

Board of Directors

Founder	Mrs. Diane Winbush
Administrator	DeVaughn Winbush
Secretary	Kenneisha Coe
Financial Officer	Clifford Watkins

The National Extraordinary Professional Women

Celebrating
WOMEN
TRANSFORMING
LIVES

Welcome

We would like to welcome you to The National Extraordinary Professional Women.
We implement many tools, tips, resources, and empowerment to meet the needs of women.
We hope that you will find the necessary fulfillment in which you are
seeking for your business and social life.

The National Extraordinary Professional Women

Celebrating WOMEN TRANSFORMING LIVES

Mission

Our mission is to provide training, education, resources, tools, and
Empowerment to build and enhance the development and
Growth of your business. To impact the lives of those women
Who have challenges in their social lives.

The National Extraordinary Professional Women

Celebrating WOMEN TRANSFORMING LIVES

Services

The National Extraordinary Professional Women
Provide services for women in healthy living,
Spiritual development, social impact, business,
Marketing, Financial growth, and more.
You can access our company in many ways as follows:

Our radio broadcast: "Women Who Rock with Success"
(www.blogtalkradio.com/womenwhorockwithsuccess)

Our Website: www.extraordinarywomens.com

Email: Info@extraordinarywomens.com

Phone: (901)290-3975

Twitter: @women4coaching

LinkedIn:
https://www.linkedin.com/profile/public-profile-settings?trk=prof-edit-edit-public_profile

The National Extraordinary Professional Women

Advertising Opportunities

We welcome advertisers to build their brands and business.
If you are interested in advertising on the radio broadcast, you can submit a request on our website. After
your ad has been approved, you will be permitted to submit
your audio file to us in an mp3 format.
The radio show host can also announce your advertisement.
On our Women's radio broadcast, we don't
accept religious
gains,
spiritual therapy,
quick rich schemes and pitches for our clients and customers. Your website
and information will be followed through to
make sure that you indeed provide these services.

Our shows may range from 15- 60 minutes per show.
View our price range on the next page.
You will receive one free airing if you
advertise three consecutive times on the show.

National Extraordinary Professional Women

Celebrating
WOMEN
TRANSFORMING
LIVES

Advertising Rates
For Show & Vendors

15 Minutes Air Time Show $25.00 for announcement

30 Minutes Air Time Show $50.00 for one announcement

45 Minutes Air Time Show $75.00 for two announcements

60 minutes Air Time Show $100.00 for three announcements

Vendors: Live events 1 hour event $50.00
Vendors: Live Events 2 hours $75.00
Vendors: Live Events 3 hours &100.00
Vendors: Live Events over 3 hours $100.00

All prices are subject to change without notice

The National Extraordinary Professional Women

Disclaimer

Vendors: all vendors whom participate on our online or live virtual events must register to be a part with the events in the time noted on the scheduled event. Payments for booth must be submitted in a time manner and before on the due date.

Refunds: All vendors will receive a refund if an event is canceled on our part. If you cancel your registration for a reason which you have; there will be no refunds. All sales and registration fees are final. This also includes the radio broadcast.

Clean Up: Once the event has event you are responsible for removing all of your material which you brought to the event.

Meals: There will be occasions in which we will bring refreshments for the vendors. This doesn't apply for all vendors. You will be notified before the event if their will or will not be refreshments.

Emergencies: If there is an emergency in the facility in which we are occupying, you must adhere to the facilities rules, policies, and evacuation plan. If you exit without following their rules, any accidents will be solely on the vendor.

Personal Property: We are not responsible for any loss damaged, or stolen properties. All vendors are responsible for securing their items and merchandise.

Professional Attires: All vendors are asked and required to dress in a professional manner.

Code of Ethics: Professional conduct is expected at all times. If there is a client whom has a disagreement with your services, you may ask them to leave your booth. But any time you are allowed to yell, curse or scream back at the attendants.

Sexual Abuse or Misconduct: If any misconduct or sexual harassment occurs while you are at either of our events, please report this immediately so we can remove and rectify the problem.

Surveys: We ask that you will finish the event by submitting a survey for the event on our website.

Appreciation: we appreciate and welcome your business.

Sponsorship: we welcome those whom may want to sponsor our event. You may submit your information on our contact page.

The National Extraordinary Professional Women

Celebrating WOMEN TRANSFORMING LIVES

A Letter from Our Founder

Women are to encourage one another for growth and stability. This company will help you to get the exposure in which you need to grow your business. I have been in positions where there was no help until I had to make the transition to network and partner with others for growth and change. It will not be easy. Business has its challenges. But you were made for this change in your business. This is why God has you there to make that change. If you ever feel stuck, just take a break and regroup yourself and go back in with those boxing gloves on. Did you know that it was meant for you to win, to accomplish, to achieve, to be that boss, ceo, entrepreneur, that business owner? What are you waiting on? Go get your dreams back. Happy Networking and growth

The National Extraordinary
Professional Women

Notes

_____
_____
_____
_____
_____
_____
_____
_____
_____
_____
_____

_____

My Journal

Celebrating
WOMEN
TRANSFORMING
LIVES

Record your Networks

Name of Business	Owner	Phone Number

Name	Business Owner	Phone Number

Name	Business Owner	Phone Number